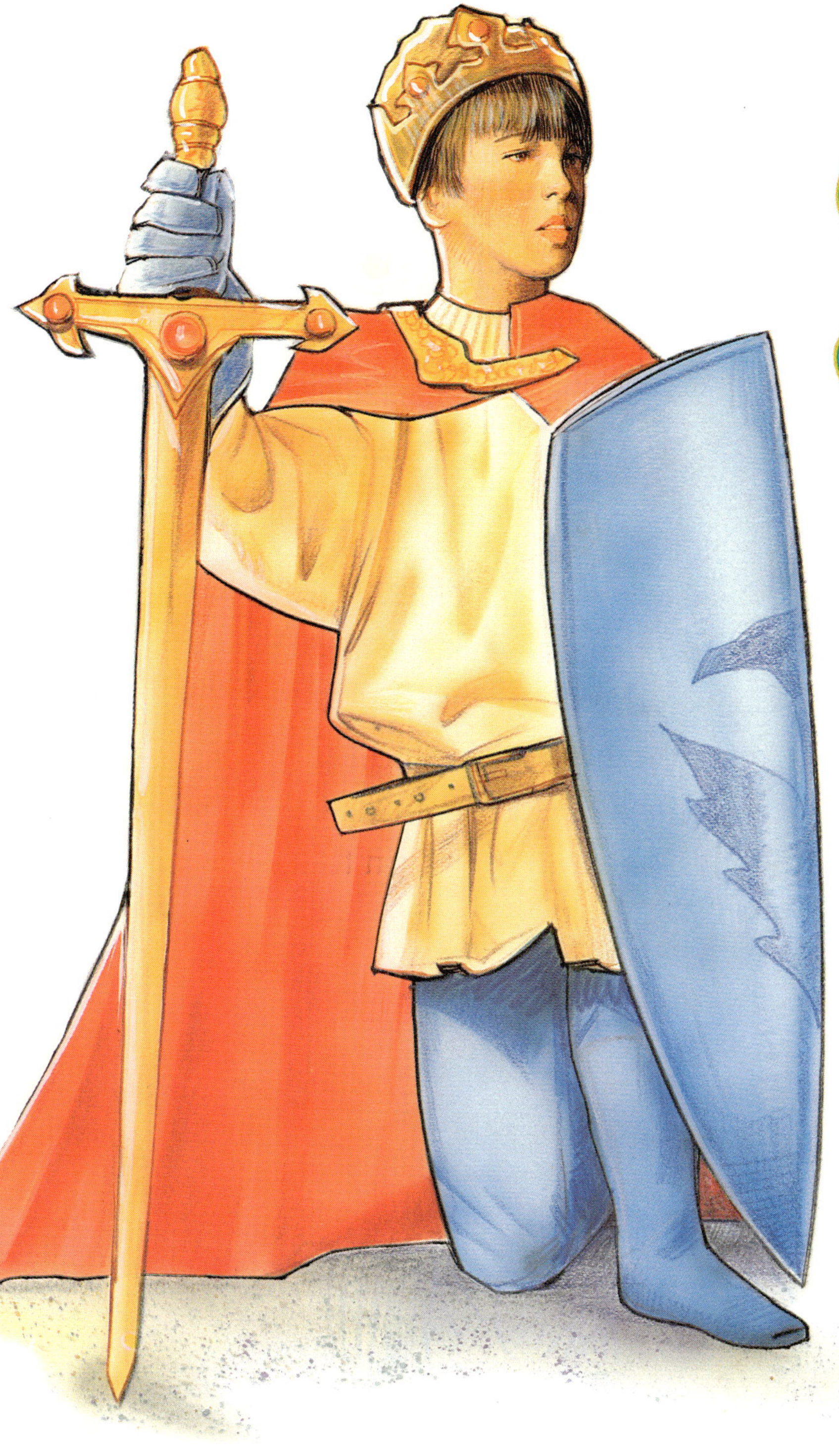

King Arthur

Tales of the Young King

EUGENE PAWZCUK

Text
CONNIE BRIM

Editor
NORMAN SHRIVE

Designer
DAVID LUKAS

Cyril Hayes Press Inc.
3312 Mainway, Burlington, Ontario L7M 1A7
One Colomba Drive, Niagara Falls,
New York 14305

In Britain in days gone by, there lived a wondrous enchanter called Merlin. Merlin possessed special powers. He could appear and vanish at will. He could read the stars and understand the secrets of nature. He could look into the future and into the hearts of men. No wonder that the King of the land, the powerful and strong Uther Pendragon, followed the advice of Merlin the enchanter.

Now, wars overtook the land when the fierce Duke of Cornwall tried to take the throne from Uther. In a mighty battle the Duke was slain. When Igraine, the beautiful widow of the Duke, made peace with Uther, they fell in love, and Igraine became Queen. With her came Morgan Le Fay, a strange little girl who, even at an early age, was skilled in the black arts of witchcraft and well-versed in the hidden secrets of nature.

Time passed, and there came a day when a son was born to Uther and Igraine. On this day Merlin appeared in Uther's chamber and said, "You are now a mighty king and feel great happiness because you have an heir to your throne. But things will not remain as they are. I know it would be best for you to let me take the child to the true and gentle knight, Sir Ector. There he will be safe and loved." And because he loved and trusted Merlin, Uther gave the child to him. Little Arthur was wrapped in a cloth of gold, and at dusk Merlin secretly carried him to the home of Sir Ector.

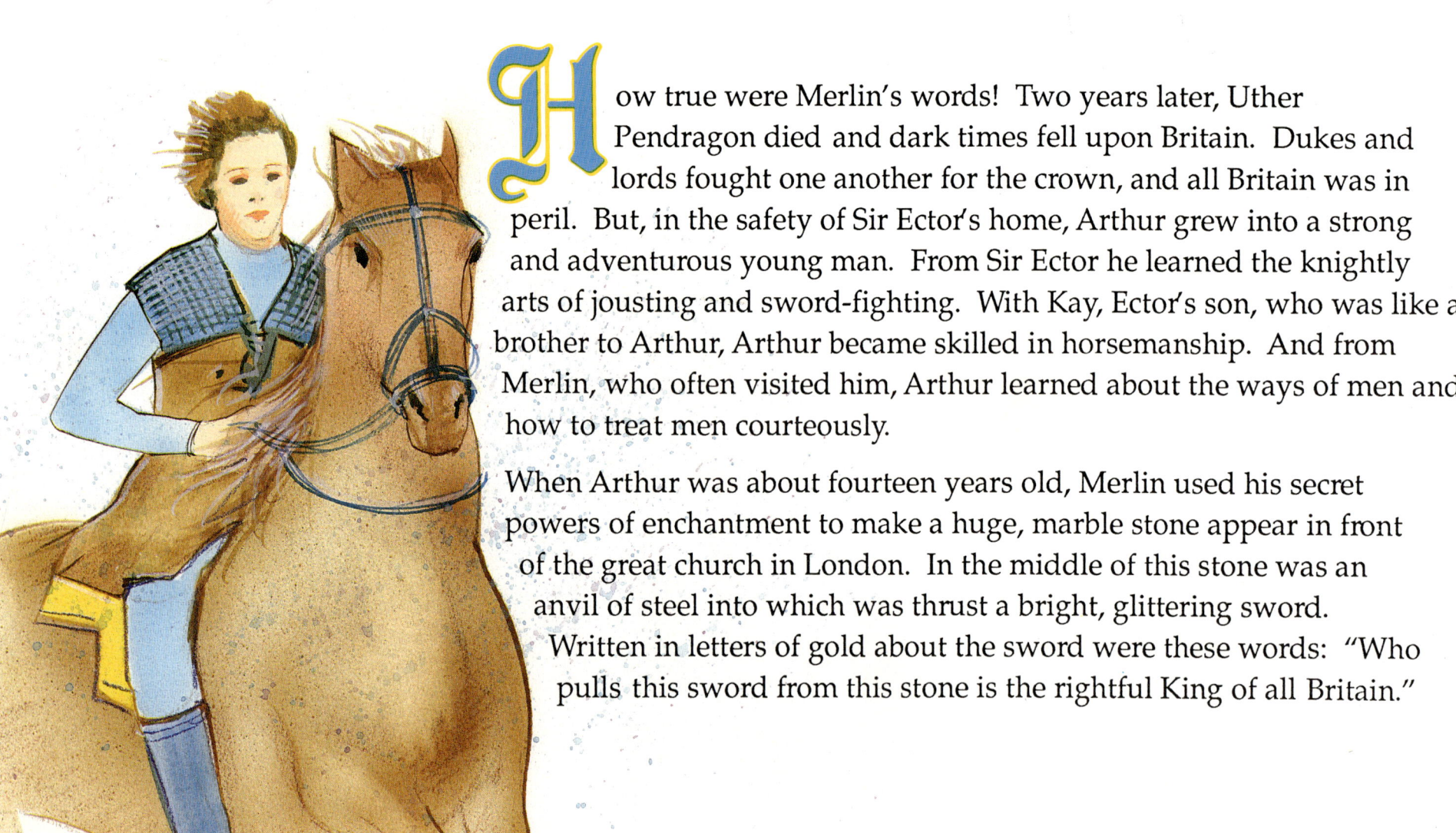

How true were Merlin's words! Two years later, Uther Pendragon died and dark times fell upon Britain. Dukes and lords fought one another for the crown, and all Britain was in peril. But, in the safety of Sir Ector's home, Arthur grew into a strong and adventurous young man. From Sir Ector he learned the knightly arts of jousting and sword-fighting. With Kay, Ector's son, who was like a brother to Arthur, Arthur became skilled in horsemanship. And from Merlin, who often visited him, Arthur learned about the ways of men and how to treat men courteously.

When Arthur was about fourteen years old, Merlin used his secret powers of enchantment to make a huge, marble stone appear in front of the great church in London. In the middle of this stone was an anvil of steel into which was thrust a bright, glittering sword. Written in letters of gold about the sword were these words: "Who pulls this sword from this stone is the rightful King of all Britain."

The people marveled when they saw the stone, and many tried to draw forth the sword. But all of them failed. Soon after, the Archbishop of Canterbury announced a Great Tournament. Knights from all over Britain came to London to test their skills and courage.

Among those who rode to London were Sir Ector, Sir Kay and young Arthur. Kay had only lately been knighted and eagerly wanted to show his skills at the Great Tournament. But, in his eagerness, he had forgotten his sword. Kay asked Arthur to ride back and get it. Arthur swiftly galloped back to the inn. There, the inn was locked because everyone was at the Great Tournament. Arthur rode back to London, and at the great church he saw the sword in the stone and decided to take it for Kay.

Arthur went up to the stone and easily drew forth the sword from the anvil. Arthur quickly took it to Kay, but when the people at the Great Tournament saw him, they cried out for him to be their king for they knew only Arthur could draw the sword from the stone.

Arthur was crowned, and he promised to rule justly and wisely. He established peace in Britain. Everyone rejoiced because King Arthur was noble and strong and because there was order in their land.

One day, after Arthur had ruled for only a short time, he rode alone in the forest, hoping to find an adventure. And an adventure he soon did find! He had not ridden very far when he came to a fountain guarded by a strange knight. "No one," said the mounted knight, "passes by this place unless he fights with me." Both Arthur and the strange knight charged at each other with so much force that they shattered their lances. Both of them now drew their swords and fought on foot. Their sword-fighting was fierce, and both fought until they were weary. Then, by chance, Arthur's sword broke. Just when the strange knight was about to be victorious, Merlin appeared and said, "Strike not that knight for he is the rightful King of Britain." At these words, the strange knight dropped his sword and asked Arthur's forgiveness.

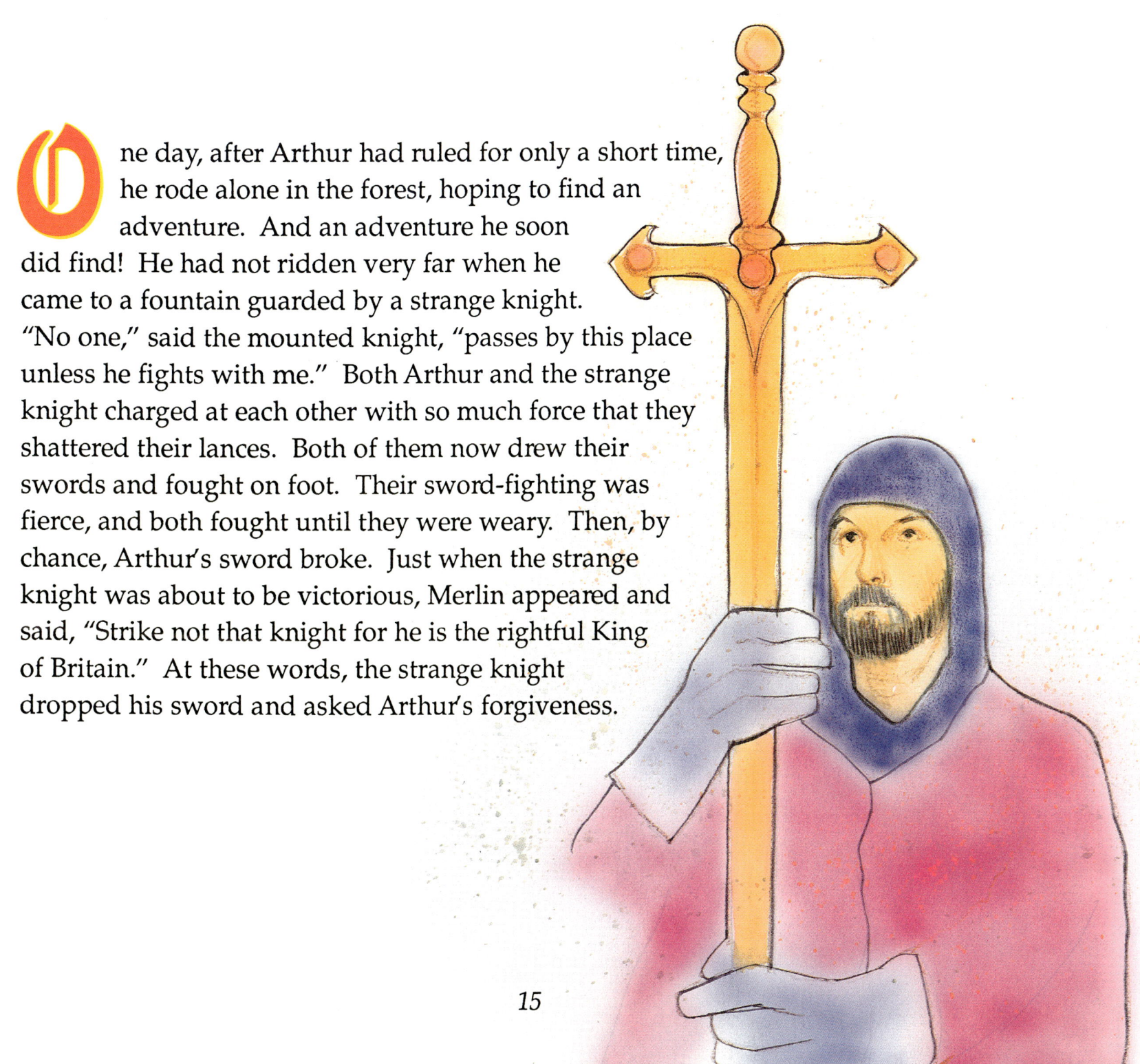

Then Arthur and Merlin departed from the fountain and rode a long distance. They came to a lake. Arthur looked across the water, and in the middle of the lake he saw an arm, clothed in white silk, holding a sword and scabbard, decorated with gold and jewels. As he looked, he saw a lady rising from the lake.

"This lady," said Merlin, "is called the Lady of the Lake. She will come to you, Arthur, and offer you the sword and scabbard. Take them; they're yours. But use them wisely."

Arthur was amazed by what he had seen, but he politely greeted the wondrous Lady of the Lake. "This sword," she said, "is called Excalibur. It is mine, but I give it to you as a gift." And she gave the sword and the scabbard to Arthur and then she was gone, vanishing into the waters of the lake.

Arthur turned to Merlin. "Tell me, Arthur," said Merlin, "which do you like best: the sword or the scabbard?"

"The sword," said Arthur, and Merlin laughed.

"Excalibur is a wonderful sword, but the scabbard is worth ten of the sword. While you wear it, you will lose no blood nor be sorely wounded. So always keep the scabbard with you."

Arthur promised Merlin he would protect Excalibur and the scabbard. A short time later, thinking it was a good idea, yet not telling Merlin about it, Arthur sent Excalibur and the scabbard to Morgan Le Fay, who was his half-sister and a sorceress.

Morgan Le Fay did not like Arthur. Though she spoke nicely to him, she did not want him to be king. Morgan secretly wanted her good friend, Sir Accolon, to be king, because she loved him and not her husband. So, when she received Arthur's scabbard and Excalibur, she decided to use them to hurt Arthur.

Arthur and Accolon were very dear friends. Neither of them had any suspicion of Morgan's plot against Arthur. One day the two men were hunting together and, after going through a deep forest in pursuit of a deer, they reached a wide river. They sat down on the bank to rest, but it was late, and they wondered if they would be able to return to Camelot before dark.

At that moment Arthur saw a barge on the river, brightly decorated with silk awnings. Arthur and Accolon boarded the barge, which was lit by a hundred torches. Twelve maidens appeared from nowhere, as if by enchantment, and greeted Arthur and Accolon by name. They led them to a table filled with food and drink. After the dinner was over, the maidens led Arthur and Accolon to a cabin and wished them good night. Because they were tired from the chase, they fell asleep immediately.

When Accolon and Arthur awoke, they were not on the barge. The barge had been an enchantment by Morgan as part of her plot to destroy her half-brother. Accolon awoke to find himself alone, lying on the grass beside a path. Arthur awoke to find himself in a dark dungeon, surrounded by the cries of other prisoners.

After a time, a damsel with a torch came into the dungeon and spoke to Arthur. "How are you?" asked the damsel.

"In an unpleasant adventure," replied Arthur.

"To free yourself from it," said the damsel, "you must fight for the lord of the castle, Sir Damas, against his brother, Sir Ontzlake."

Because Sir Damas was an evil man, Arthur did not want to fight for him. But he agreed provided all the other prisoners were also freed. Meanwhile, Accolon saw Morgan's dwarf, who had come to tell him that Morgan wished him to do battle with a certain knight. And because the fight was to defend her honor, she had sent the dwarf to bring to Accolon Arthur's sword Excalibur and its scabbard.

At that moment (and this was all part of Morgan's plan), Sir Ontzlake rode up and asked Accolon to be his champion against his evil brother.

The next day Arthur went to do battle for Sir Damas, while Accolon did so for Sir Ontzlake. Because they each wore borrowed armor, neither knew who the other was.

The fight was long and terrible. Accolon, with the wonderful Excalibur, sorely wounded King Arthur. Though Arthur fought with great strength and skill and wounded Accolon deeply, he seemed unable to do any real damage, and Accolon lost not a drop of blood. This was, of course, due to Accolon wearing the magical scabbard of Excalibur. Suddenly, with one last valiant effort, Arthur seized Excalibur and its scabbard from Accolon, and threw him to the ground.

When each man had removed his helmet, they were amazed at how easily they had been tricked. Accolon was grief-stricken at nearly having killed his king.

Arthur readily forgave him, and together they went to a nearby monastery to have their wounds healed. Arthur recovered quickly, but Accolon died.

When Morgan Le Fay heard of her friend's death and of Arthur's knowledge of her plot, she vowed to get Excalibur and the scabbard again. She quickly departed from Camelot and, after riding all night, came to the monastery at dawn. "I am Morgan Le Fay, King Arthur's sister," she said to the porter, and he allowed her to visit the sleeping Arthur. Arthur held Excalibur in his hand, but the scabbard was on the floor.

Morgan took it and swiftly rode away. When Arthur awoke and found the scabbard gone, he asked a servant if he had seen anyone. Upon discovering it was his wicked sister, he quickly rode out from the monastery. But, though Arthur searched far and wide, in forests and valleys, by lakes and rivers, he could not find his half-sister or the scabbard. By her witchcraft, Morgan had changed herself into a stone. Only when the search was over did she change her shape again and return to her own land. There, she made a strong fortress and lived alone, ever cursing Arthur and ever plotting his downfall.

The End